earth-circuit

earth-circuit

poems by
iyra e m maharaj

earth-circuit

Dryad Press (Pty) Ltd
Postnet Suite 281, Private Bag X16, Constantia, 7848,
Cape Town, South Africa
www.dryadpress.co.za/business@dryadpress.co.za

Copyright © poems iyra e m maharaj
All rights reserved

No part of this book may be reproduced or transmitted in any form or by any electronic or mechanical means, including photocopying and recording, or any other information storage or retrieval system, without prior written permission from the publisher or copyright holder

Cover design & typography: Stephen Symons
Copy Editor: Helena Janisch
Set in 9.5/14pt Palatino Linotype

First published in Cape Town by Dryad Press (Pty) Ltd, 2023

ISBN 978-1-991209-17-7 (Print)
ISBN 978-1-991209-18-4 (Electronic)

Visit www.dryadpress.co.za to read more about all our books and to buy them. You will also find features, links to author interviews and news of author events. Follow our social media platforms on Instagram and Facebook to be the first to hear about our new releases.

Dryad Press is supported in the publication of this collection by the Khula Cape Foundation whose generosity and commitment to literature and the arts is gratefully acknowledged.

Even though you won't believe me
my story is beautiful
And the serpent that sang it
Sang it from out of the well

– Leonora Carrington, *The Complete Stories of Leonora Carrington*

CONTENTS

creation

the witch in glass wind cycles	3
cooling	4
gold leafing	5
violet	6
bedbug	7
october	9
procreation	10
heart flood	11

death

thoughts of a woman applying lipstick	15
the drifter	17
insomnia	19
the jailer	20
rolling and unrolling	23
a luta continua	25
psalm 0	26
i prefer birds in cages	27
witch glorious	28
in the gloaming garden	29
one night	30

evolution

ouroboros	35
kintsukuroi	37
earth-circuit	38

mendel's garden	40
angry feminist love dreams	41
datura	42
babylon	43
succubus	44
japanese mermaids	47
mary	48
himalaya	50
the tower	51
Acknowledgements	55
Notes on poems, epigraphs and quotations	56

creation

the witch in glass wind cycles

in the south
seven mothers before me
lay birds and bricks and myrrh
under storm lights and cold water

like some unwatched wick
i broke and bore
like a midnight doorbell
a snake in a letterbox
the maddening answer to
prayer

the witch in glass wind cycles
shuttled me awake
in a warbling pitch
no one could remember

and i was birthed
pawing from webs and mud
blushed swollen
and cradled in blotting clay

violet

who is the one with a full heart?
slim roads between rolling green fields
always crawl beneath one another
and i stretch out *are we there yet?*
behind golden sheets
my mother laughs—i yawn again

who is the one with emptiness?
bare trees that smell like rain
always slice past this dusty car window
and i dream anxiously
behind my phone
everyone groans as we leave the province again

who is the one with apologies?
red-hill rocks with tall lake birds
always spiralling downwards
and i roll down my window and hum
behind a hymn
my friends awaken—it's winter again

who is the one with the morning?
the mountain streaked across a violet sky
always moves as we circle it
and i stretch out the salty air
i smile and i smile—
this time i won't leave myself behind

bedbug

i stretch out my hand to see if god
will come to touch it
i feel my wrist prickle and think
is that it? an itch?
well if god's a bedbug then frankly
i'm a little relieved

i wouldn't know what to say to an enormous
electric angel—something ethereal or humanoid
of fire blood lightning—some shadow of broad wings—
i'm far more comfortable
with an invertebrate—

maybe he's a man with hard bones and soft lips
that i drown down the wet drain
maybe i glow
pressed lightly under the moon and pretend god
is the candle wax i dip my finger in

i curl up my sticky hand and close my eyes
i see reeds
i see dust

if it doesn't matter what god looks like
let me be the shrike that kisses god
on her wet red lips
let me stir hot coffee and pray god is insoluble

if i'm his likeness
then god is just a girl with post-coital blues
this bug biting my skin
a reminder to wash my sheets
and he'll probably be dead soon

october

under a sky of dangers lie lovers like fallen fruit
smashed to the ground crushed into each other
and dripping—aches travel from my heart to my
thighs—fears slither from my mind to my tongue
tasting timeless thoughts of overripe skin

have i not scratched you deeply enough in my
daydreams? let this cosmic glow tilt me away
from you—let the stars balance us out
let's for once let life breathe through its own lungs

procreation

if you ever tasted Cain's wine
you'd disappear into the wilderness
wade through strokes of a dull powdered sun
aching to fill cracks in the earth

i'm taken back further
than the time of no saviours
when i could paint my
breasts with the blood of beasts
when the only electricity that flowed was
a curse branding my skin

i drink in this dust
and exhale the black sky
the time of no time
no stars and no doubt

heart flood

we meddled with time rings
when i asked you how your
tectonics could shift the circuitry
of my blood pipes
how you could blow hot sand
into rain rocks in the devil's red

what is a mood?
an angry southern man like a flood
when i first saw you
my waterfall witness fell
like a butterfly like an elephant

but now i've stolen the meddler's cane
as cliffs tip him into the sprawling sea
'til i die i will spring rain rocks open
'til i live i will never know you

death

thoughts of a woman applying lipstick

i trace colour on my lips the way
ladies in Cosmo blow their husbands

if we   meet in a life after this one
i hope   you'll dance with thunder
and sell   your soul to the desert
for a chance   to marry me under
chandeliers of   moonlit rain for
the chance to stitch my   soul onto
yours with wet threads and   blue
petals crushed and plastered   on
a portrait hanging in   our library

the tragedy is not   unrequited love
it is the universe   whose troops of
stars shoot   mockingbirds & scoop
their   blood into thick pottery jars
it   is that nobody deserves sorrow
born   from a dream they thought
they had   the right to have and
some poets   in my tattered books
opened my eyes   to love: do love
a woman, love a   man love her
hard love him deeply   and shout
out *je t'aime à la folie* in   an old
tourist house from the top   of a
wooden staircase—bite   hard into
a roasted chocolate   coffee bean
smile one   movement at a time
envision   skin—for true love's kiss
is a smouldering cocoa aphrodisiac

and   the poets that died of broken
bones   suffered less than those of
shattered   hearts—swollen souls
that were   told only to adore love
and to love   the ones whose stars
crept into their   lungs and flew
out of their mouths   in song

as   rare   as   an   ideal   world
as precious as earth—   swimming
through a milky   mess of light
this is the event   that set my soul
burning on   a comet dripping
down a   candle spinning into the
wind   since thinking of you shifts
my   jaw open wider driving the
shaft   of my berry lipstick further
into my   skin and here lies the
real difference   between my time
and yours: that   i believe in living
on love and time   but too much
romanticism of romance   is a strain
on your neck

i'll go on walking into   the sun
i'll go on dreaming of   datura but
i'll never take it   i'll go on asking
why the one   thing i sincerely felt
had to jolt   up my lip bruising my
gum   lashing a smooth berry pink
stain   across   my   face

the drifter

I

i tried to tell you about ghosts
but you wanted to walk with wings
across gleaming midnight

>   *how marvellous this stone stands*
>   *the kaleidoscopic temple*

II

you drilled below sacred stone
for mountain fog and amazon leaves
like clues to the map of an exceptional life

>   *i love this torrential literature*
>   *this racing heart*

III

i cannot sleep—
i keep dreaming
Ezekiel's visions leave me breathless

>   *surely the Creator*
>   *hides some synaptic answer*

IV

i've lost my ability to fly
as the tender sky reddens with clouds
these sights of life give birth to death

> *i'm leaving you behind*
> *in crimson dusk and bone*

V

i tried to warn you about ghosts
but you wanted to run forever
across a reddening sky

insomnia

in dirt i buried my ancient brain
to drown and forget itself again

here you are with bellows
here you are with trumpet stars
here you gnaw at your leash
but quiver and howl
when it snaps free

as if my mind
my sour old mind
needed another wrinkle

the jailer

I

the room smelled of paint and chocolate
a stain that won't fade
no matter how vigorously you grate
no matter how deeply you peel

> *mothers don't cry when boys run towards large tanks*
> *fishermen don't weep when they return home with nothing*
> *these were my forced whispers in her ear*

II

ticking antiques and wooden furnishing
a land flowing with silk and money
was no consolation
pain still trickled through
i swear

> *i told her that i don't kiss women on the mouth*
> *and by day left her to her thoughts*
> *that's when she finally listened and stopped her crying*

III

i have sorely learned
that violence makes
man a god

> *she substituted her sobbing with writing*
> *i planned to toss her diary into the crackling fire*
> *when she wasn't looking*
> *i am telling you the truth*

IV

i longed to run away on raw hands and feet
in the dark blue night
instead i watched him
slowly begin to pay attention

> *she made friends with the cooks*
> *and kissed the servant boy in the woods after dark*
> *swam naked in the river at dawn*
> *all sorts*
> *glistening with peace*

V

sometimes he'd let me smoke in his room
other times he snarled and barked
this is the whole truth

> *i am—was—already very wealthy*
> *there was no ransom*

VI

i kissed him on the mouth
and he snapped at me

days after kissing me back
i could hear him pacing

> she grew bony and lifeless
> and looked cross when i amused myself
> holding her up as we waltzed across the carpeted floor
> nothing but the truth

VII

i think
in his mind
he planned to let me go

> the thought of letting her go never crossed my mind
> she ran free all by herself out the window
> and down the piping in the dead of night
> i have the proof
> i was furious

VIII

i'll visit him every Christmas
so help me god

rolling and unrolling

the dreams i dream are otherwise enchanted
like the earth we exploit
to build resorts
made to look like the earth
the finest grass door you ever hid behind
from luminous desires
that tip into a glow

       and you dreamed he traced your lips
       with the black clay you abandoned
       take me back into crumbling soil

this time the thoughts i think tremble and shake
like money i paid
to watch a woman dance like god
between two pianos
the finest impression i ever clung to
a broken mother who sang my heartbreak into myself

       and you dreamed of photographs he took
       through salt-washed eyes
        i've already walked these evening avenues—this time

the prayers i pray roll and unroll
like my slithering skin
when i think of you
and for a moment my atmosphere blended into the ground
like bones liquefied absorbed

        and who wrote the lover's bible—
        tattooed *timing was here?*
         you dreamed he touched your lips
         and your salt-washed eyes
         linger

but the dreams i dream are still awake
like golden time melting in my veins
a ticking song
a pumping clock
as endless as the joy glowing
in my eyes and in yours

a luta continua

some kid at school burned a painting
of red-clothed colonials
to let the state know
we are awake
we will not take this anymore

i wish i had the fucking spine
to light my path to freedom
my self-esteem is not made
of the same leather
you stretch around your shoulders
it's a bird's feather picked off the ground

i cannot say *it is what it is*
because you make me unfixable
you make it what it always will be
i will always pass the lighter on
because my hands quiver
under pressure

and your conscience
(oily slivers of paint
from some forbidden suburb)
is unapologetic—
framed to a wall

psalm 0

dear everlasting
your pulse stills trembling mountains
your hands spread apart the earth and squeeze out life
you are sovereign in every thought you ignite
through every doubt i carry on the brittle wings of prayer
do i deserve these blessings of silver seas and mercy
of purple skies and love? i'm a sinking rat
drowning slowly smoothly in bubbling fat—
but you are the universe
and you overwhelm my heart
how often have i cried out to you
kneeling at the shore of heaven?
your breath melted my cloud and when it rained
healing fell dropping heavily onto sand like ecstasy

but if i know anything it's this:
i wish i loved god the way i love you
why do i treat him like a poltergeist
when you are the disturbing vibration under my bed?
in the beginning i was a cell
then i was two then five thousand
and he fed me a dream
then a legion of demons
and he chained himself in with us
i walked streets of gold streets of dust
but like an arrow in my flesh you were a ghost
plunging into me then leaking out
he was there when you left—
is still here when you leave me burdens to pick up
the puddles of water i cannot grasp
like bee stings i try to scrape away

i prefer birds in cages

i prefer birds in cages
underfed and sickly thin

i prefer pollutants
pandora parasites
and proliferation

i am the truth and i
prefer creaking cobwebs
crawling across the wall

i prefer my dogs alive
whimpering on forever

witch glorious

~ for Uyinene Mrwetyana

witches oiled
plaster papers on gleaming stone
under gold moons or white comets
whispers keep wicks burning

witches simmering
while men in the shade watch them
pop like bubbles one by one

witch glorious
birds in her eyes and lights on her thighs
billows into a quiet place
worker smiling
spills her onto the carpet

witches thundering
dangling off a bridge
highway motorists reach for their phones
that frame large red letters:
where is she?

in the gloaming garden

in the gloaming garden i enter a clearing
and sit at the base of the sacred statue

her feet pinned together nearly fish-tailed
an ensnared siren groaning for salt

i slurp up this folklore like yellow broth
and mud-bellied i wait but hear no answer

i am stuck here decrepit with chimeric pain
this version is not in my translation

it cannot be deciphered by any glass-stained
mystic nor his webbed paper codex

these antarctic floes in my veins come
in thunderclaps while the garden siren sleeps

surely this pain is new territory
surely this is raw ungoverned rock

in the quiet bramble below
my white-eyed reptile watches and waits

one night

one night
i prayed against the changing colour of the sky
scratching my insides i woke up in hell
where hair melds to scalp and fingernails lodge
in the walls of the heart where teeth protrude
through eyeballs and where everyone tells you
not to cry because *you deserve better*

tonight
(this black blood-midnight) there is a wild chill
along the back of my neck—the soft of
my thighs—ice runs down in droplets and
blades into my spine

now
i can hear the wind in the trees
the sound of god changing things—i creak
open the door prowling light-footed
to the corner to find myself cracked open
like a vase

i stretch out my hand pick myself up
walk out of the room and never look back

evolution

ouroborous

dear sad people
i always believed that the sun would turn purple
the day humanity learned to glow

but lately my warm wooden library turned cold
in the summer i'd pick up the heaviest explanation
of evolution and smile at it like a proud amphibian

in the winter i'd pray to a stagnant universe
forget i'd evolved in a dream—
i walked through the first testament

where ocean lapped up coarse sand
and transfigured into bones
standing tall and cracking open a footpath

it never ends someone said to me
but then it does—did i belong in your world?
you write so many letters to your pills and lovers

priests and ghosts—i chose to write my own letter
to a raised razor nightmare running and raw
a woman peeling herself to sleep

in a dream—the old testament sent me a witch
and the witch sent me a sparrow
to unfurl the summer that slept on my lap

the sparrow sent me a muse
who trembled into Egypt and
turned serpents into stars

the muse sent me a book—cell to bone
to bristlecone pine tendon to asteroid—
that i had written myself

it never ends and then it does
and glows with the bursting
violet of dawn

kintsukuroi

today we learn to love ourselves—
there is someone sitting above the universe
who leads us to a desert of dry bones

he wipes off our aching crusts
picks up our cracked ribs
and fills our empty spaces
with gold

and swimming through our veins
trickling down our lungs
we find our reddest rose

earth-circuit

when the sun sinks the earth's skin crawls:

I

i wonder if this awkward creature
would notice me the way i notice him
so lonesome at his throne
i stare after him longingly
(and yet)
he never realises that i'm the one
who basks in his brilliant beams
if only he knew how much brighter he could burn
(with me)
he'd light up the universe

II

i heard him speak of thirst once
the quenching lust of the stars had run dry—
so that night i brought a bottle
of acid
(how it gleamed in his glow)
handed it to him wrapped in taffeta ribbons
chanting *curdling joy*
on my gurgling boy
i love his eyes now
clouded white like milk from a poisoned tree

...tura

my love sways slowly in the grip of the beast
crooked gates rusting to the ground
leaking paradise from the pores of her feet

oozing like sap from arcane trees
he whips through dirt with nail and bone
my love sways slowly in the grip of the beast

bending her neck to sour teeth
with knotted hair tangled in burning branches
she leaks paradise from the pores of her feet

over stony canyons his snapping wings beat
a terrible light flooding the valley
my love sways slowly in the grip of the beast

spine ready to crack skin leather-loose to peel
open like a rose in the white morning
leaking paradise from the pores of her feet

her reptilian hatching now complete
i am too big for this garden
my love sways slowly in the grip of the beast
leaking paradise from the pores of her feet

III

when the sun sinks the earth's skin crawls:
hyper-responsive circuitry
retrieving—coiling up
from bloom to bird to brainstem—
closing and caving inwards

mendel's garden

the garland devil lets his daughters roam sour gardens
squeezing lemons across their necks like perfume
sisters six mock the seventh for being recessive
the malignant seed in the *Pisum* patch—
but she will not yield *i can rub old wine*
and apple slime deep into my pores she says
but lemons—i shall never wear lemons

the garden favours the dominant daughters
leaving the garland devil to roam their necks
under tended lemon trees

angry feminist love d[...]

dear lord jesus that woman
smelled like bubble gum
and cherry-broth lipstick
frothing out of apple chapel c[...]
under pink city smog

i couldn't see her face
but i wondered if her tongue ta[...]
as sweet as the fruity juice
that drips out of her

today my heart rots as soft as bl[...]
but thank you for a ten-second v[...]
of something far riper than a ma[...]

there isn't time to let the world b[...]
in its own sludge—pick a religion
we hate the smell of warm milk
and throbbing mammals
who suckle their way out of thoug[...]

my breasts shall not be used for mi[...]
my breasts shall be for the cherry-b[...]
she is goddamn delicious

babylon

this strange sunlight
this pulsing slime
creaking off a wooden bridge
into the wet and glistening
i love you like a lightning bolt
licking up a milky mountain

we trip over poisoned roots
when the earth lets down her hair
by the far fucking (soul) sucking stars
your lips are wild like the devil's
and your eyes gleam
a shimmering bathsheba witness

and babylon
    babylon
    babylon

roses run down my thighs
run down my thighs

succubus

in the   pale blue
         dark blue
         cold blue
afternoon
sits an old ghost
of a man

the blue sun heats
he stares ahead
with veiled
    grey eyes
and withered hands
motionless

at the dusty shack
slapped together—wood gate porch—
sits the man
    the ghost
you'll never see what i see

he blinks
and in a
      flash
his heart loose powder—
shakes
unmoving gazing
through wooden frames
his eyes meet theirs
there is no life

III

when the sun sinks the earth's skin crawls:
hyper-responsive circuitry
retrieving—coiling up
from bloom to bird to brainstem—
closing and caving inwards

mendel's garden

the garland devil lets his daughters roam sour gardens
squeezing lemons across their necks like perfume
sisters six mock the seventh for being recessive
the malignant seed in the *Pisum* patch—
but she will not yield *i can rub old wine*
and apple slime deep into my pores she says
but lemons—i shall never wear lemons

the garden favours the dominant daughters
leaving the garland devil to roam their necks
under tended lemon trees

angry feminist love dreams

dear lord jesus that woman
smelled like bubble gum
and cherry-broth lipstick
frothing out of apple chapel chimneys
under pink city smog

i couldn't see her face
but i wondered if her tongue tasted
as sweet as the fruity juice
that drips out of her

today my heart rots as soft as black plums
but thank you for a ten-second whiff
of something far riper than a man

there isn't time to let the world balance
in its own sludge—pick a religion and eat it
we hate the smell of warm milk
and throbbing mammals
who suckle their way out of thought

my breasts shall not be used for milk
my breasts shall be for the cherry-broth woman
she is goddamn delicious

datura

my love sways slowly in the grip of the beast
at crooked gates rusting to the ground
leaking paradise from the pores of her feet

oozing like sap from arcane trees
she whips through dirt with nail and bone
my love sways slowly in the grip of the beast

bending her neck to sour teeth
with knotted hair tangled in burning branches
she leaks paradise from the pores of her feet

over stony canyons his snapping wings beat
a terrible light flooding the valley
my love sways slowly in the grip of the beast

spine ready to crack skin leather-loose to peel
open like a rose in the white morning
leaking paradise from the pores of her feet

her reptilian hatching now complete
i am too big for this garden
my love sways slowly in the grip of the beast
leaking paradise from the pores of her feet

    fear   through his
                  (mangled)
                  (ghost)
                  (blue)
                  body
but he sits still
and still sits

flash again
        white shack blue shack
        white house blue shack
        white shack blue house
faulty film
crackling in silence
        in heat

he still sits
he sits still

dried thoughts
hang over the porch
like meat—pressed salted
he stares
beyond the witching realm
    to   pale
             old
             cold
blue

milky shadows
cover his eyes
and in a
flash

snakes gather
around his feet
he still sits
he sits still

the final blink
reaching his edge
his feet bleed
in spinning
> (dusty)
> (lusty)
> (light)

he looks again
the porch is bare

his tired hands
reach up to the cold
> pale
> blue blue sky

clawing with nails
to pull it down
like a shutter

you said there'd be a devil here

the   ghost man
          old   man
          pale man
          cold man

still sits
sits still

japanese mermaids

i spit salt trinkets out my mouth
sky gods crouch over the ocean
fishing for japanese mermaids
their golden grins like shamans

i inhale a pale bloodied sun
that tips against the evening grey
a smiling mermaid heaves forward
infant teeth jut from decay

moving fast, a slithering fish
kisses my tongue, my milky eyes
drown along the temple dirt road
as i glimpse a shrinking sky

mary

this is the plan
before you follow the dirtmap
                the skylamp
                the cocktalk
feel your feet on the ground
in the heavy predawn

the sky and i watch you
with pale sympathy
and anticipation

your route is prearranged
in the evening i'll talk with God
while life-sized boxes dressed in flowers
float away on the back of ceremonial
            carving
            swallowing
            smoking

His silence will be my answer
as it has been
for aeons

and i've marked the spot
here
Joseph will meet you under the yellow light
(just walk with me a moment)

do you see the other side?
the golden plan that weighs you down
aching your feet your breasts your spine

is nothing but His meddling magic—
it is blood water and wine
treason and death
unspeakable pain
for a scriptural shadow
a magician
another dark boy crucified

mark my words
cathedrals will rise red and murderous
men will transfigure into swine
and fruit will swing
in the dead of night

change your direction
ignore the king the cities and the footpaths
summon bells alabaster and horns

here is a river—
you hold the power now

himalaya

it took an ache of an age
to climb into terrestrial hide

but the day i found you
was the day sun devils dropped dead

a bipedal knock
on their sloping sycamore laws

to climb into milk
and boil with the white-bellied calf

we bit pages off
archaic books to chew them like cud

and swallowed them—
a tectonic second coming

my snow-capped shadow
you are the amber morning

i am the wrong kind
of soil tossed in uneven heaps

you are the root that
crawls into me still and swells

the tower

in the land of the dead the air feels loose
buildings tighten with preoccupied chirps
trills over coffee cake chatting ratting
over laundry fruit flies floating in blue
planters jutting—everything is the same
(nearly) green umbrellas paint—but no wind
not the slightest breeze

indoors the blind queen sleeps on paper maps
of the americas while her thighs run
dreams of finding bones in the house lifting
tablecloths screaming swallowing hair white
as fingertips into her mouth crying
wake up! but she keels over
choking on her tongue

upstairs a boy plays and twists the marble
knife to his stomach ready to split his
abdomen open like milkweed
further i prod a door with one finger
to the woman staggering underneath
an oozing another door and another woman—
something is wrong—there is no breeze

in the land of the dead, oxygen coils
weak curdled—i think of those women—
will they die? will i? can you still die here?
outside the gathering crowds gaze upwards
a crooked clock tower gleams beneath
the scowling white ball of steam shivering
i hear the ground rising with horse thunder

in mist the sun sinks fast: silken faces
commanding slender guns—i feel urgently
the pull and prowl of beautiful men
here at the end of the world—something moves above
the choking queen the staggering women
the dead children—my stomach churns
water pours from my mouth and i must leave

have you ever seen the devil? a voice
like an angry spirit on stone and grass
below we vibrate a rippling blanket
unravelling in fear—then it comes the quiet horror—
he seems a man the handsome face pierced
to the tower top red on stone
he smiles stretching his arms like a covenant

the apex of a blood ritual
as a wind begins to howl

Acknowledgements

For their love, which sustains me, I am thankful to my parents Pravin and Clara, my sister Zaineta and my partner Andy.

Thank you to Simon van Schalkwyk for his guidance and advice and to Michèle Betty for her invaluable feedback and commitment to bringing this collection to publication.

Thanks are also due to the editors of *New Contrast: The South African Literary Journal*, where versions of some of these poems first appeared.

iyra e m maharaj

Notes on poems, epigraphs and quotations

Page vii
Even though you won't believe me
my story is beautiful
And the serpent that sang it
Sang it from out of the well
Leonora Carrington, *The Complete Stories of Leonora Carrington* (New York: Dorothy, 2017.)

Page 25
A luta continua is Portuguese for *the struggle continues* and was the rallying cry of FRELIMO during Mozambique's war of independence against Portuguese colonial rule.

Page 47
The title Japanese Mermaids is inspired by Iwase Yoshiyuki's photo series titled 'Japanese Mermaids'.

OTHER WORKS IN THE DRYAD PRESS LIVING POETS SERIES

AVAILABLE NOW

Night Transit, P. R. Anderson
Dark Horse, Michèle Betty
Star Reverse, Linda Ann Strang
Transcontinental Delay, Simon van Schalkwyk
The Mountain Behind the House, Kobus Moolman
In Praise of Hotel Rooms, Fiona Zerbst
catalien, Oliver Findlay Price
Allegories of the Everyday, Brian Walter
Otherwise Occupied, Sally Ann Murray
Landscapes of Light and Loss, Stephen Symons
An Unobtrusive Vice, Tony Ullyatt
A Private Audience, Beverly Rycroft
Metaphysical Balm, Michèle Betty

OTHER WORKS BY DRYAD PRESS (PTY) LTD

Palimpsests, Chris Mann
River Willows: Senryū from Lockdown, Tony Ullyatt
missing, Beverly Rycroft
The Coroner's Wife: Poems in Translation, Joan Hambidge
Unearthed: A Selection of the Best Poems of 2016,
edited by Joan Hambidge and Michèle Betty

Available in South Africa from better bookstores nationwide, and online at www.dryadpress.co.za and internationally from African Books Collective at www.africanbookscollective.com

www.ingramcontent.com/pod-product-compliance
Lightning Source LLC
Chambersburg PA
CBHW070615170426
43200CB00012B/2700